W9-AMR-428

SEP 2011

DATE DUE

NOV 2 2 2011			
NOV 19 2012			
NOV 2 5 2013			
JUN 2 4 2016			
NOV 2 8 2017			

Jr. Graphic Colonial America

THE FIRST THANKSGIVING

Andrea P. Smith

PowerKiDS press

New York

Published in 2012 by The Rosen Publishing Group, Inc.
29 East 21st Street, New York, NY 10010

First Edition

Editor: Joanne Randolph
Book Design: Planman Technologies
Illustrations: Planman Technologies

Library of Congress Cataloging-in-Publication Data

Smith, Andrea P.
  The first Thanksgiving / Andrea P. Smith. — 1st ed.
      p. cm. — (Jr. graphic Colonial America)
  Includes index.
  ISBN 978-1-4488-5187-4 (library binding) — ISBN 978-1-4488-5212-3 (pbk.) — ISBN 978-1-4488-5213-0 (6-pack)
  1. Thanksgiving Day—Juvenile literature. 2. Pilgrims (New Plymouth Colony)—Juvenile literature. 3. Massachusetts—History—New Plymouth, 1620–1691—Juvenile literature. 4. Thanksgiving Day—Comic books, strips, etc. 5. Pilgrims (New Plymouth Colony)—Comic books, strips, etc. 6. Massachusetts—History—New Plymouth, 1620–1691—Comic books, strips, etc. 7. Graphic novels I. Title.
  F68.S586 2012
  974.4'02—dc22
                                                                    2011001668

Manufactured in the United States of America

CPSIA Compliance Information: Batch #PLS1102PK: For Further Information contact Rosen Publishing, New York, New York at 1-800-237-9932

CONTENTS

MAIN CHARACTERS

William Bradford (1590–1657) Second governor of the Plymouth Colony and signer of the **Mayflower Compact**. He wrote a book about the Pilgrims called *Of Plymouth Plantation*.

John Carver (1576–1621) First governor of the Plymouth Colony and signer of the Mayflower Compact. He died during his first **term**, less than a year after he became governor.

Myles Standish (1584–1656) A soldier who met the Pilgrims in Holland. He helped the Pilgrims and guided them on **military** matters.

Samoset (1590–1653?) A leader of the Abenakis who learned English from fishermen in Maine. He was the first to welcome the Pilgrims.

Squanto (also called Tisquantum) (1580–1622) A Patuxet Native American who lived in England for many years. When he returned to Massachusetts, he became an **interpreter** for Massasoit.

Massasoit (d. 1662) The chief of the Wampanoag tribe of Native Americans. He agreed to a peace **treaty** with the Pilgrims so they could protect each other from other Native American tribes.

THE FIRST THANKSGIVING

IN ENGLAND DURING THE 1600S, EVERYONE HAD TO BELONG TO THE CHURCH OF ENGLAND. A GROUP OF PEOPLE DISOBEYED THE LAW, THOUGH, AND WORSHIPPED IN SECRET. THEY BECAME KNOWN AS PILGRIMS.

ON SEPTEMBER 6, 1620, THE *MAYFLOWER* SET SAIL FOR THE NEW WORLD. THE JOURNEY WAS LONG AND HARD.

I FEEL SEASICK.

I WISH WE COULD GO UP ON THE DECK.

QUICK, TOSS HIM A ROPE!

HELP!

AFTER MORE THAN TWO MONTHS AT SEA, THE PILGRIMS MADE IT TO PLYMOUTH BAY.

THIS WILL BE OUR NEW HOME.

THE FIRE WAS ONLY ONE OF THE PROBLEMS THE PILGRIMS FACED THAT WINTER. HUNGER AND SICKNESS ALSO TOOK THEIR TOLLS.

OF THE 102 PILGRIMS WHO ARRIVED IN THE NEW WORLD, 52 DIED THAT FIRST WINTER.

AFTER MUCH TALK, THE PEACE TREATY WAS FINISHED. BOTH SIDES AGREED NOT TO HURT THE OTHER SIDE AND TO HELP EACH OTHER OUT WHEN THERE WAS TROUBLE.

IN THE FALL, THE PILGRIMS HELD A HARVEST CELEBRATION. THEY ASKED THE WAMPANOAGS TO JOIN THEM.

PLEASE CELEBRATE THE HARVEST WITH US.

WE WOULD BE HONORED.

I LOVE ROASTED DUCK.

THERE'S A FAT ONE. QUICK, FIRE!

WONDERFUL! PUT IT OVER THERE.

THIS DEER IS OUR GIFT FOR THE CELEBRATION.

YOU'RE DOING A FINE JOB GRINDING THE CORN.

I HOPE COOKING THE **HASTY PUDDING** IS LESS WORK THAN MAKING IT.

ME, TOO.

ADULTS SANG AND DANCED.

THIS IS SO MUCH FUN.

GENTLEMEN, WE'VE MADE IT THROUGH SOME BAD TIMES THIS YEAR, BUT I BELIEVE THE WORST IS BEHIND US.

WE MUST GIVE THANKS FOR OUR **SURVIVAL.**

AND FOR OUR WONDROUS HARVEST.

THIS HARVEST CELEBRATION IS CONSIDERED THE FIRST THANKSGIVING.

TIMELINE

1534 — King Henry VIII separates the Church of England from the Catholic Church.

Summer 1617 — Pilgrim leaders talk to the Virginia Company about moving to the New World and forming a colony.

Spring 1620 — Pilgrim leaders make a deal with London investors so they can pay for their trip.

September 6, 1620 — The *Mayflower* sets sail for the New World.

November 9, 1620 — The *Mayflower* reaches Cape Cod, Massachusetts.

December 9, 1620 — The Pilgrims find a suitable place to build their colony near Plymouth Bay.

Winter 1621 — Fifty-two members of the colony die from hunger and sickness. John Carver dies and William Bradford becomes governor.

January 1621 — The Pilgrims build the first meetinghouse in Plymouth.

March 16, 1621 — Samoset visits Plymouth for the first time.

March 22, 1621 — The Pilgrims and the Wampanoags sign a peace treaty.

Fall 1621 — The Pilgrims hold a celebration for their first harvest.

1863 — President Abraham Lincoln makes Thanksgiving a yearly holiday to be celebrated on the fourth Thursday in November.

GLOSSARY

abundance (uh-BUN-dens) A large amount.

fertilize (FUR-tuh-lyz) To put something in soil to help crops grow.

hasty pudding (HAY-stee PU-ding) Cornmeal mush.

interpreter (in-TER-prih-ter) Someone who helps people who speak different languages talk to each other.

Mayflower Compact (MAY-flow-er KOM-pakt) An agreement that stated the way the Plymouth Colony would be governed.

military (MIH-luh-ter-ee) The part of the government, such as the army or navy, that keeps its citizens safe.

negotiate (nih-GOH-shee-ayt) To talk over terms for an agreement.

New World (NOO WURLD) North America and South America.

palisade (pa-luh-SAYD) A fortification made from a row of pointed stakes set into the ground.

pneumonia (noo-MOH-nya) An illness that people can get in their lungs.

preserves (prih-ZURVZ) Keeps something from being lost or from going bad.

routine (roo-TEEN) When someone does something the same way over and over.

sparse (SPAHRS) Having only a few of something.

survival (sur-VY-val) Staying alive.

term (TURM) A period of time that an elected official can serve.

treaty (TREE-tee) An official agreement, signed and agreed upon by each party.

INDEX

WEB SITES

Due to the changing nature of Internet links, PowerKids Press has developed an online list of Web sites related to the subject of this book. This site is updated regularly. Please use this link to access the list:

www.powerkidslinks.com/JGCO/thanks